Prisons and Penal Reform

Tessa
BLACKSTONE

Prisons and
Penal Reform

Chatto & Windus
LONDON

Published in 1990 by
Chatto & Windus Ltd
20 Vauxhall Bridge Road
London SW1V 2SA

A CIP catalogue record for this book
is available from the British Library

ISBN 0 7011 3554 9

Photoset in Linotron Ehrhardt by
Rowland Phototypesetting Ltd
Bury St Edmunds, Suffolk
Printed in Great Britain by
St Edmundsbury Press Ltd,
Bury St Edmunds, Suffolk

Acknowledgments

I should like to thank Stephen Shaw, Director of the Prison Reform Trust, for his help, advice and constructive suggestions on this monograph. I am grateful to Professor David Downes, Robert Hazell and Vivien Stern for their helpful comments on an earlier draft. I am also grateful to Jill Emery for typing the manuscript. Finally I should like to thank John Eatwell for his encouragement and support throughout its production.

Introduction

'The mood and temper of the public in regard to the treatment of crime and criminals is one of the most unfailing tests of the civilisation of any country' –

Winston Churchill, House of Commons, 1910

BRITAIN'S PRISONS are institutions of which we should be ashamed. They are absurdly expensive, yet scandalously inhumane. For the most part they are in old or decrepit buildings, but even where the buildings are new they are often badly designed. They absorb large amounts of manpower, yet typically lock inmates in their cells for many hours a day. They are overcrowded and unhygienic. They enforce idleness and encourage helplessness. They certainly punish; they hardly reform.

These judgments are not controversial. They reflect the views of most people in the Home Office who now have or have had responsibility for prisons, of many of those responsible for administering the prisons, and of key groups of professionals who staff our penal system such as prison governors, probation officers and the Prison Officers' Association. Yet the number of people we incarcerate in these dreadful institutions has grown year on year. We now have a considerably higher proportion of our population in prison than all our European neighbours, exceeding not just Scandinavia, France, Belgium, Holland and Germany, but even Spain, Portugal, Greece and Turkey. Our detention rate is proportionately well over twice as high as that of many other countries in Europe.

Why are we doing this? Why are we spending so much money on a penal policy which is so singularly unsuccessful? Why do we rely so heavily on a form of punishment which is so costly to the society at large and to the individual concerned? Why have we been so inept in changing sentencing patterns? Why have the various alternatives made so little impact on the numbers in prison? Why are the conditions in our prisons such a disgrace? Part of the answer is the serious failure of our senior politicians to provide a proper lead. No one doubts the difficulty of reforming the system, but with courage, conviction, imagination and common sense it could be done. These attributes seem to have been sadly lacking amongst the politicians in charge, especially over the last ten years.

Some part of their unwillingness to act probably rests on their perception of popular attitudes towards crime. Deviant behaviour which involves breaking the law cannot be ignored. In all societies sanctions are applied in the interests of maintaining social order. Society demands that they should be applied, and it is right to do so. Many crimes have victims, who deserve to be protected from further victimisation. Some crime is motivated by greed; some is selfish and thoughtless; some is a function of stupidity. Some can be excused as a consequence of events beyond the control of the individual concerned, or a function of hopelessness and despair. But where there are no genuine mitigating circumstances those who have committed offences must expect, if they are caught, that something will be done to demonstrate that their behaviour is unacceptable. The problem is that politicians, particularly Conservative politicians, appear to believe that the electorate wants those who have been found guilty of committing crimes to be dealt with in the harshest way possible.

There were more resolutions about law and order tabled at the 1988 Conservative Party Conference than on any other subject. But evidence suggests that people do not want *just* to get tough on crime. Above all they do not believe that sending so many of those convicted of crimes to prison is desirable. The Home Office itself carried out two surveys of public attitudes in the early 1980s. The vast majority of those questioned were in favour of reducing the prison population.

With opinion poll data as clear as this on his side, the Home Secretary should be able to persuade the Prime Minister and his other colleagues that their commitment to value for money should be applied to the penal system as well as to the rest of the nation's public services. The attitudes of the tabloid newspapers, which have condemned desirable changes such as reductions in maximum penalties, should not be allowed to determine government policy.

The Government's Record

Increased resources and increased powers

SINCE 1979 the government has invested heavily in all the law and order services and extended the powers of the courts. Yet the annual number of offences recorded by the police has grown by well over 1 million since Mrs Thatcher became Prime Minister. Law and order is, along with defence, the only part of the public sector in which the objective has been to spend more. Spending on the criminal justice system as a whole has increased from about £2 billion in 1979/80 to an estimated £5 billion in 1988/89, an increase of about 50 per cent in real terms. The police, prisons, probation services and the courts have all benefited from the government's heavy spending on the criminal justice system. An extra £1.6 billion has been committed towards total Home Office spending, most of which is to be spent on expanding the prison system and increasing local authority spending on the police. In cash terms, the Home Office's central government spending will have risen by 60 per cent, an increase without parallel elsewhere in the public sector. There are now 14,000 more police officers than there were in 1979. This is broadly equivalent to an extra four provincial forces. The policy of recruiting more civilians to undertake certain support tasks has also added to the effective strength of the police. The number of probation officers has grown by 6 per cent, and there has been a spectacular rise of nearly two thirds in the

5

number of probation ancillaries, mainly working on community service schemes and in probation day centres.

However, the most staggering rise has been in the number of prison staff, with an increase of over 50 per cent between 1979 and 1991. This reflects the government's massive investment in the prison system. The largest prison building programme for 100 years will add at least 28 new prisons to the system. Many more places will be provided by the redevelopment of existing establishments. The 1988 public expenditure settlement resulted in an extra £610 million over the next two financial years to allow for the further expansion and acceleration of the building programme, providing an additional 10,000 places over the next three years, with about that number again by the mid-1990s. The total cost of the building programme is now budgeted at over £1 billion.

Based on projections of the future size of the prison population, there should by the mid-1990s be a broad equivalence of the number of prisoners and the number of places to accommodate them. However, such projections have not proved very accurate in the past. Despite the prison building programme, prison overcrowding has consistently spilled over into police cells. At one time in 1988 over 1,500 prisoners were being accommodated by the police because no room could be found in the gaols. Just after Christmas 1988 the Home Secretary issued a triumphant press release trumpeting that the police cells had been cleared. The 'clearance' lasted less than a week, and by early January 1989 over 300 prisoners were being held in police cells, many of them no more than six foot by six foot and with no natural light.

Both the Criminal Justice Acts of 1982 and 1988 increased the powers of the courts. In its approach to sentencing, the government has had a twin-track policy; arguing for 'tougher' sentences for violent crime while suggesting that non-violent offenders should be kept out of prison. This policy has done nothing to reverse the UK's poor record in the international league table. In contrast, the country which used to be our closest rival – West Germany – has cut its prison population by 20 per cent in the past four years. Indeed, the proportion of offenders who are imprisoned has increased substantially during the Thatcher years; 21 per cent of adult men and 8 per cent of adult women convicted of indictable offences are now sent to prison, compared with 17 per cent and 3 per cent a decade ago. Yet only one person in every five imprisoned each year has committed offences involving violence, sex, robbery or drugs.

The government has also done little to control the grotesque disparities in sentencing practices of courts in different parts of the country. A convicted offender is roughly twice as likely to be sent to prison by magistrates in Oxford as in Cambridge, or in Manchester as in Liverpool. An accused person is *ten* times more likely to be remanded in custody by courts in Dorset than in Bedfordshire or Hertfordshire. A report from the Children's Society has shown that 16 per cent of all juveniles in custody are sent there from Greater Manchester alone.

Increased Crime

The number of notifiable offences recorded by the police reached almost 3.9 million in 1987, compared with 2.5 million in 1979. Some 94 per cent of the 1987 total were crimes against property: burglary, theft, fraud and forgery, and criminal damage. Only 5 per cent were crimes against

7

the person, a category which encompasses violence, robbery and sexual offences.

The growth in the crime rate has been an embarrassment to the government, although the official crime figures are known to be a poor indicator of the total volume of crime. Many offences are not reported to the police, and even if reported are either categorised incorrectly or not recorded at all. Moreover, the rate at which offences are reported/ recorded is not constant over time. The growth in household insurance (claims for which are dependent upon the offence being reported to the police) and the spread of telephone ownership are just two reasons why the rate of reporting may have increased. Equally, variations in the rate of recording may be a result of differing priorities and complement levels of individual police forces.

It is probably fair to say that the official police statistics of recorded crime considerably *underestimate* the level of offending and *overestimate* its annual rate of increase. Notwithstanding these difficulties with the police statistics, and the fact that they exhibit considerable fluctuations in the short term, the government has made much of the fact that figures for 1988 were lower than for 1987. This was the first reduction in the 12-month total since 1983. And despite the fall in total crime, the figures for violent crime have continued to grow. It remains to be seen whether the overall decline will prove lasting. Demography is certainly contributing to it. The peak ages for offending are 14 for females and 15 for males. Juvenile crime has been falling for several years because of the fall in the size of this age cohort. In the mid-nineties, however, the size of this age group will start rising again.

Government Policy

Despite the part which 'law and order' played in the 1979 election campaign, within two years William Whitelaw was planning a measure (supervised release) which would have cut the prison population by 7,000. Leon Brittan cut up to 3,000 from the prison population overnight by changing the rules on parole. Douglas Hurd cut the number by about 2,000 by introducing 50 per cent remission on sentences of up to twelve months. Other changes have had the reverse effect. For example, tougher sentences for violent crime have been advocated and the sentencing powers of the courts extended. By way of illustration, the 1988 Criminal Justice Act increases the maximum penalty for carrying a firearm in the course of crime to life imprisonment and introduces a measure enabling the prosecution to appeal against a lenient sentence in certain circumstances.

In contrast, three Conservative Home Secretaries have exhorted the courts to avoid the unnecessary use of custody for non-violent crime. The most remarkable statement of the government's policy on non-violent crime and its attitude towards the use of custody appeared in the 1988 Green Paper 'Punishment, Custody and the Community'. Noting that the reformative impact of sharing a cell with two other criminals is likely to be limited, the Green Paper states: 'Imprisonment is not the most effective penalty for most crime. Custody should be reserved as punishment for very serious offences, especially when the offender is violent and a continuing risk to the public.' The government is also on record as admitting that the power of the criminal justice system to influence the crime rate is limited (*Criminal Justice: A Working Paper*, rev. ed. 1986).

However, while hoping to minimise the use of custody,

the government has not been willing to introduce statutory restrictions upon the discretion of the courts except in relation to juveniles and young adults. Instead, it has sought to encourage the confidence of the courts in non-custodial measures. Thus, new guidelines have been issued to the probation service governing community service orders, and a new, more punitive and controlling emphasis is proposed for probation practice generally. These initiatives, such as electronic surveillance, have had a negative reception from probation officers.

Electronic tagging is widely perceived as a gimmick. Unfortunately a taste for gimmickry has been one of the characteristics of the government's penal policy. The 'short, sharp shock', originally introduced when detention centres were first set up in the late forties, was repromoted as a no-nonsense approach to youthful offending, only to be abandoned when it became clear that such regimes were regarded with distaste by magistrates but with some enthusiasm by the young delinquents themselves.

The government has also sought to make political capital out of other 'initiatives' like Neighbourhood Watch. Although over 60,000 such schemes have been set up, the vast majority are moribund. Even in those areas where they are active, the impact upon crime is unproven.

An emphasis upon private responsibility for crime prevention has been a distinguishing feature of the Thatcher years. In part, this reflected a wider ideological shift. In part it appears as if government, recognising that increased spending on conventional measures will not be effective in reducing crime, has turned to crime prevention almost in desperation.

Like Neighbourhood Watch, great things have been claimed for the government's crime prevention initiative.

However, the truth is that the government has no overall picture of crime prevention activity – how much is being spent, or what works under which circumstances.

Another major flaw in the whole government strategy is that people are more powerful – if more expensive – deterrents to crime than technology. It appears to be the case that, as caretakers reduce vandalism, so concierges reduce burglary and car-park attendants reduce car crime. But if employing people such as caretakers is more effective in preventing crime than any amount of hardware or improved street lighting, this is hindered by the financial hurdles which the government has placed in the way of such crime prevention measures. Government restrictions on local authority spending have reduced the number of worthwhile crime prevention schemes which might otherwise have been introduced.

The other trend in government policy is the privatisation of services. The 'Punishment, Custody and the Community' Green Paper holds out the possibility of private sector involvement in a new sentence of punishment in the community. However, the area which has attracted most public interest is the possible privatisation – or, more accurately, contracting out – of certain types of prison. The Green Paper 'Private Sector Involvement in the Remand System', published in July 1988, proposed privately-managed bail hostels and remand centres together with a privately-run escort service. Up to 40 companies and consortia have already been invited to tender for contracts to design and build, but not to manage, new open prisons and remand centres. The Green Paper indicated that a decision had in principle already been taken in favour of some private management. It is now widely believed that the first private remand centre will open some time in the

11

first half of the 1990s. The escorting of prisoners from gaol to court and back by private contractors also looks a certainty.

Breaking the monopoly of the Prison Officers' Association is one of the reasons behind the government's proposal to privatise aspects of the prison service. Prisons are highly labour-intensive: staffing and related costs average over 80 per cent of total costs. For many years the system was overtime-driven, and in an effort to bring costs under control the Home Office has introduced an ambitious pay and productivity deal, under the title 'Fresh Start'. By August 1988 every establishment had switched to Fresh Start, the deal guaranteeing greatly enhanced basic wages in return for an anticipated saving in staff hours of 15 per cent by April 1989.

However, the effects of Fresh Start have been patchy. Regimes for prisoners have not generally been enhanced as had been hoped, and staff shortages have developed, particularly in the hard-pressed local and remand prisons. Industrial action has been taken at several prisons and the POA has enforced unilateral ceilings on the number of prisoners in many gaols. Conflict between the union and the Home Office has become an endemic feature of the prisons scene.

The rights of prisoners have also gone largely unrecognised. A proposal from HM Chief Inspector of Prisons for a Prisons Ombudsman has still to receive the support of the Home Office. There has been controversy over suicides and major incidents of prisoner unrest both in England and Scotland. Despite the massive building programme, thousands of prisoners will still be 'slopping out' in the twenty-first century. The Chief Inspector of Prisons has denounced the practice and demanded a timetable for ending it. The Home Secretary has accepted proposals but thus far has refused to predict when slopping out will end.

The government's record in the area of law and order can only be described as a sad failure. All it has done is throw money at the problem; behaving in a way which Mrs Thatcher herself deplores. Much of this money has been wasted. A number of new policies have proved unsuccessful. For example, there have been three different systems for treating young offenders, of which the most widely publicised was the unsuccessful 'short, sharp shock'. The handling of the parole system has been incompetent and inconsistent, and even the prison building programme has been the subject of serious criticism by national audit.

In December 1985, the National Audit Office issued a strongly-worded report criticising the Home Office's management of the prison building programme. Strategic planning was weak, staffing and maintenance costs of particular designs had been ignored, accommodation of the wrong type and the wrong design had been built in the wrong places, the building programme had been characterised by delay and overspending. Moreover, the NAO predicted – correctly, as things have turned out – that the building programme 'will not succeed in meeting [the] target objective of matching total available places with aggregate prison population by the end of the decade'.

Subsequently a new Prisons Building Board – including private sector representation – has been set up in the Prison Department and a new set of design briefs formulated. However, the much-vaunted 'private sector techniques' turn out on closer inspection to be little more than the less than revolutionary idea of using the same design on more than one occasion. Slippage on most new prisons continues. The Public Accounts Committee has deprecated the continuing failure to deliver new prisons on time and has rejected the Home Office's excuses as 'unrealistic'.

Government Ideology

The values that have been purveyed since the arrival of Margaret Thatcher at 10 Downing Street have not been conducive to a reduction in crime, particularly in crime against property. Opinion polls have consistently shown that the public believes that a decade of Conservative government has resulted in a more materialistic and greedy society. Attaching a high value to making money, stressing competition rather than co-operation, rewarding those who do make money, are all part of Thatcher's philosophy of life. Wealth and material possessions have become increasingly important symbols of status.

Not all can succeed in the tough competition for material success. Some of those who fail are drawn to crime, which can look like an easy way to obtain the possessions which the values of Thatcherism have turned into a *sine qua non* for a satisfactory life. They are simultaneously pushed into crime by an oppressive ethos of materialism and by the denial of legitimate means of achieving at least a modicum of material success. Because of high unemployment and low levels of educational achievement, many young people, especially young men in the inner cities, cannot get jobs and so resort to illegitimate routes to owning videos, stereo equipment, fashionable clothes and cars. This is not to excuse their behaviour; it is to try to explain it.

It would be absurd to suggest that improvements in

educational opportunity would eliminate crime amongst those in their late teens and early twenties. However, the failure of the British educational system to keep more young people at school or college after the age of 16 seems likely to have an indirect effect on crime rates. Many young people leave school at the earliest possible opportunity, even though their chances of getting a job are small. In 1981 45 per cent of 16–18 year olds in the UK were in full- or part-time education or training, close to the bottom of the league amongst OECD countries. The Swedes had achieved more than double that figure (94 per cent); and the proportions were much higher for Germany (85 per cent), USA (79 per cent), Japan (72 per cent) and France (66 per cent). By 1987 the figure in the UK had risen to 50 per cent, but it had also risen in most of the other countries as well.

The fact that benefits have been cut has exacerbated the problem. For example, social security changes which came into effect in April 1988 reduced levels of income support for young people. These were followed in September 1988 by the withdrawal of income support from most young people under the age of 18. These changes place many young people in severe financial hardship. Initially they also created barriers to the use of intensive non-custodial penalties, because offenders' attendance during normal working hours prevented them from attending youth training schemes (and hence receiving training allowances). Fortunately as a result of lobbying a change has recently been made allowing young offenders to attend youth training schemes and claim their allowances, at the same time as attending day centres as a non-custodial penalty.

The link between government social and economic policies and crime rate increases cannot be scientifically established. However, the balance of evidence suggests they have an effect. For example, the sense of helplessness caused by youth unemployment has been linked to hard-drug use, which in turn implicates some adolescents in crime who would not otherwise be caught up in it. While most industrial societies have high rates of crime, the British government must be censured for running unnecessary and excessive risks with young people's lives in the 1980/85 period when it adopted policies which trebled unemployment and blighted job prospects in inner-city older industrial areas.

It is in fact a failure, not just of the imagination but also of common sense, to assume that crime can be totally detached either from the prevailing value system or from socio-economic conditions. The government has shown little recognition of these fundamental points. Instead it has committed itself to law and order as a symbol of the strong central state. This commitment manifests itself in the prison building programme. The state demonstrates its power and authority through the expansion of penal institutions in which those who do not conform are incarcerated.

There is, moreover, a paradox in the government's approach to dealing with crime. On the one hand it devotes large sums of public money to building prisons, while on the other it is trying to offload crime prevention and some forms of the treatment of offenders onto agencies outside the public sector. In spite of large increases in expenditure the police have had notably little success in preventing crime or in clearing it up. In 1977 the clear-up rate (offences cleared up as a percentage of the total number of offences recorded) was 41 per cent. Ten years later it had fallen to

33 per cent. If the police can do little to stop crime, clearly other methods should be considered. Recent examples of this are the then Home Secretary, Douglas Hurd's espousal of the concept of the 'active citizen' as well as the promotion of Neighbourhood Watch schemes. Such schemes fit neatly into a government ideology which favours self-help and less dependence on the state, even though the schemes themselves may appear ineffective.

Privatisation

The privatisation of services previously provided in the public sector has been the driving force of government policy in many areas. Its ideological commitment to a much smaller public sector has become an obsession. Thus in July 1988 the government published a Green Paper on 'Private Sector Involvement in the Remand System' (Cmmd 434).

The paper asserts that the government 'is not at present inclined to accept that there is any overriding difficulty of principle which ought to rule out private sector involvement, provided that sensible practical safeguards are built into the arrangements'. The central issue of principle, which the paper ducks, is whether or not any agency other than the state itself can have direct responsibility for prisoners and the way they are treated. It is a view accepted by governments all over the world, notwithstanding small-scale experiments in the United States, that the coercive powers necessary to enforce the deprivation of liberty should be the direct responsibility of the state. The civil liberties of the citizen are so centrally involved in penal policy that the state cannot abrogate its responsibilities to institutions operated in the pursuit of private profit. As our greatest criminologist, Sir Leon Radzinowicz, has written: 'in a democracy grounded on the rule of law and public accountability the enforcement of penal legislation, which includes prisoners deprived of their liberty while awaiting trial, should be the undiluted responsibility of the state. It is one thing for private companies to provide services to the prison system but it is an altogether different matter for bodies whose motivation is primarily commercial to have coercive powers over prisoners' (*The Times*, 22 September 1988).

As recently as July 1987 the Home Secretary accepted this view: 'I do not think there is a case, and I do not think that the House would accept a case, for auctioning or privatising the prisons or handing over the business of keeping prisoners safe to anyone other than government servants' (Hansard, 16 July, 1987). The Home Secretary seems to have bowed to pressures from the ideologues of the right. In doing so he was risking the creation of a powerful lobby with a vested interest in a higher prison population.

As well as issues of principle, there are many practical problems associated with handing over the custody of remand prisoners to profit-making organisations. Staff employed in the care and treatment of offenders require training and experience in the skills necessary to do this work properly. No private organisation currently has such staff at its disposal. To obtain them it will have to lure them away from existing public sector institutions and embark on expensive training schemes. The former will mean paying higher salaries than the prison service, while the latter will involve high costs per trainee with none of the benefits of economies of scale. As a consequence, if private remand centres are to be properly staffed they are likely to have high costs, and to be even more expensive than existing institutions. It is likely that firms tendering for contracts will cut costs in an effort to secure the contract. The result could be remand centres with either too few staff and, as a consequence, inhumane regimes based on high technology surveillance and most of the inmates' time spent locked in cells, or poor quality staff unable to perform their duties properly.

The quality of staff in remand centres is no less important than in institutions which house convicted prisoners. Prisoners on remand often have very serious problems. Many have not adjusted to the trauma of imprisonment and the separation from family and friends. They often suffer from high levels of anxiety about the outcome of their cases. Rates of suicide are considerably higher amongst remand prisoners than convicted prisoners, and offences against prison discipline in remand centres are nearly three times higher than in local prisons. Many remand prisoners need legal advice; others need support and advice in dealing with alcohol, drugs or medical problems. Coping with remand prisoners is a complex human and organisational matter. The government's Green Paper brushes aside what would happen if things went wrong, blindly stating that contracts could be terminated quickly. In practice it would take time to terminate a contract and redistribute three or four hundred men elsewhere. In the event of a riot, existing public sector institutions would have to pick up the pieces.

Passing responsibility from state-run institutions to private contractors also raises important issues of natural justice. It must be questioned whether commercial firms and their staff should be able to influence the length of time a person remains in custody.

Conduct on remand can influence a convicted prisoner's security category, allocation to a particular prison and parole

opportunities. Moreover, remand prisoners can lose pro-
spective remission. Even if it were decided to allocate only
low-risk prisoners to private remand centres, the behaviour
of prisoners cannot always be accurately predicted.

It is almost certain that private contractors would opt for
low-risk prisoners if given the choice. This would leave the
state to deal with higher-risk prisoners where costs are
higher. How prisoners are to be allocated to private remand
centres and public institutions is unclear, but obviously
private contractors should not be allowed to pick and
choose. If low-risk prisoners are selected for them, there is
an even greater danger for such prisoners that a commercial
lobby with vested interests in maintaining current levels of
remands in custody could be created. It is of course low-risk
prisoners who should be granted bail wherever possible,
and certainly far more often than happens at present.

The ideology of privatisation rests on the government's
frequently-stated convictions about the value of healthy
competition. 'Healthy competition', however, has little rel-
evance to penal institutions. Indeed, the idea of consumer
sovereignty in the prison system would be absurd. Prisoners
are not going to be offered a choice between a commercially-
run remand centre and a public remand centre or prison, nor
will they have an effective voice to make their preferences
known, even if they have had the misfortune to sample both.
Alternatively, the State as 'consumer' has such an overriding
responsibility for the quality of the service in this case, that
the separation of supplier and consumer is meaningless.
Comparisons with local government services where contracting out has been introduced by the government are not
meaningful either. Many companies might contract for
cleaning schools or old people's homes, as the staffing and
management skills required are undemanding. Setting up

companies to run prisons with the necessary trained staff and management expertise is much more difficult.

Privately-run prisons were the norm in the eighteenth century, but the recent interest in privatisation – like that in 'tagging' – has been imported from the United States. However, even there less than 0.5 per cent of prisons are privately managed. Privatisation is likely to remain peripheral, at least for the foreseeable future. The Immigration Centre at Harmondsworth on the edge of Heathrow Airport has been privately managed since 1970. Each place costs the Home Office roughly three times what it would in a Prison Department establishment. At the beginning of 1989 the contract was switched from Securicor to Group 4, although its terms were not made public on the grounds of commercial confidentiality. This does not augur well for lower costs, adequate public accountability and increased efficiency as a result of privatisation.

The other method the government has proposed for reducing the size of the public sector in the criminal justice system is to extend the involvement of private organisations in the running of non-custodial penalties and 'punishment in the community'. The involvement of voluntary organisations in the operation of Intermediate Treatment for young offenders, and the whole multi-agency approach (involving police, probation, social services, magistrates and the voluntary sector) has been one of the government's more successful initiatives. In January 1983 the DHSS made £15 million available to fund intensive Intermediate Treatment schemes to be developed by voluntary organisations. A total of 110 such projects were eventually established, subsequent research showing that they had a significant impact on the rate of custodial sentencing of juvenile offenders.

However, what is proposed in regard to 'punishment in the community' is very different. The proposal is that while the probation service (or some new quango to be created) would have overall responsibility for punishment in the community, it would not itself provide all the elements. Voluntary organisations might take on some, private security firms others (such as the monitoring of curfews).

Organisations dealing with potentially highly-charged situations involving offenders who have been given non-custodial sentences should be publicly accountable. The probation service and social service departments can be called to account if they are negligent. It is difficult to see how private sector security firms can be made accountable in the same way. To give private companies details about individual offenders and presumably the right to enter private houses also raises serious issues of civil liberty. It is questionable too whether involving more than one agency in supervising an individual order makes much sense from a practical point of view. If probation officers have to devote time and effort to monitoring progress on the different elements of an order and to keeping various different participants aware of any difficulties, they will have less time themselves to work directly with offenders. Staff in private organisations will have to be trained; inexperienced and untrained staff should not be put in a position where they could, for example, recommend breach proceedings to a probation officer in charge of an offender.

The government's obsession with privatisation is re-inforced in the context of penal policy by its difficulties with the trade unions concerned. The Prison Officers' Association (POA) has often backed much-needed re-forms to the prison regime, but it has also uncompromis-ingly pursued its own vested interests for many years. It has often stood in the way of a more rational deployment of staff in prisons and has sometimes been a barrier to fairer and more humanitarian treatment of inmates. Some of the blame for poor relationships with the prison officers must be attached to poor management and to conditions in prisons which result from the government's failure to get a grip on policy, particularly in relation to sentencing. The government has also alienated the National Association of Probation Officers (NAPO). It has shown little understanding of the demanding nature of probation officers' work in helping and rehabilitating offenders, and has failed to recognise just how important it is to raise the morale and status of probation officers if there is to be a successful transfer to more non-custodial penalties. Without the support of the profession it will be difficult to bring about such a transition. NAPO's negative response to the government's proposals on 'Punishment, Custody and the Community' reflects the extent to which probation officers have lost confidence in the government. Clearly they doubt whether the political will exists to pursue alternatives to custody. However, the probation service is not without its faults as the recent Audit Commission inquiry into its work has demonstrated. It needs to be better managed, with clearer targets and objectives. Undue defensiveness from NAPO is also unhelpful.

Populism and Punishment

One of the striking characteristics of Thatcher's premiership is its populism. The right-wing tabloid press frequently screams for tougher penalties for convicted criminals, described as 'monsters' and 'beasts' who should be put away for the rest of their lives. Believing that these newspapers reflect their readers' views, as well as moulding them, ministers respond accordingly. In some cases their own personal views may fit quite neatly with those of the *Sun*, in others they certainly do not, but ministers lack the courage to say so, mindful, perhaps, of Willie Whitelaw's mauling at the Conservative Party Conference in 1981, when he adopted a more progressive approach to the treatment of crime. Instead, an ideology which is punitive in intent is purveyed. This leads ministers into uncomfortable contortions on matters such as the use of non-custodial sentences.

Thus the government's Green Paper 'Punishment, Custody and the Community' constantly emphasises punishment rather than retraining, rehabilitation and reform. As the criminologist Professor Terence Morris has aptly put it: 'By its very title it presumes that non-custodial forms of disposal *ought* to be punitive, whereas it has been received wisdom for more than a generation that the objectives of such sentences as probation and more recently of community service should be identified as rehabilitative; the very need for the offender's assent would seem to suggest that these are not punishments, *per se*, but rather contractual forms of social expiation.' The central dilemma for the government is how to put across proposals for more use of non-custodial sentences such as Community Service Orders or probation, whilst at the same time maintaining its macho image of 'getting tough on crime'. It has tried to resolve this dilemma by emphasising the retributive nature of non-custodial sentences. But in doing so and also in focusing on gaining the confidence of sentencers, it may undermine those sanctions which actually reduce the risk of further offending. As the Prison Reform Trust maintains in its comments on the Green Paper: 'Punishment for its own sake can hardly be said to encourage self-reliance; indeed it may cause the very resentment which makes re-offending more rather than less likely . . . In particular the emphasis on regulating the movements and leisure activities of offenders through tracking, electronic monitoring and curfews may have a similarly disabling effect to the helplessness and dependence so often engendered by imprisonment.'

Nevertheless there are arguments for placing some emphasis on punishment in relation to non-custodial sentences. For many young offenders, doing community service every Saturday for a year will certainly seem like punishment. And if it helps to reduce the numbers in prison, it may be justified. Thus if the electorate, magistrates and judges can be persuaded that there are alternatives to prison, and that these alternatives are not 'soft on crime', the government may have a case. Where it certainly does not have a case is in the use of wild and aggressive language about offenders, which has the effect of talking up the prison population. References by the Home Secretary to the 'moral brutishness of thugs' and by the Prime Minister and the Minister of Sport to football hooligans in language more suitable for describing violent gangsters than irresponsible, excitable and childish young men under the influence of drink, are not helpful. If in speech after speech ministers overstate the anti-social nature of crime and exaggerate the toughness of the sanctions needed to control it, they have only themselves to blame when judges respond by sending more people to gaol. If ministers want to reduce the numbers in custody, and 'Punishment, Custody and the Community' makes it clear that they do, they must alter their own behaviour as well as asking other people to alter theirs.

The State of the Penal System
Who goes to prison?

Those who go to prison are not a random section of the population. They are overwhelmingly young and male. They come mainly from the most disadvantaged group in the community: the urban poor. They are frequently unemployed, poorly educated and totally untrained. Many are black. They and their families have often been the victims of crime themselves. Their childhood will not uncommonly have been marred by neglect or abuse. They have sometimes grown up on the margins of society. Adult prisoners are often homeless with little or no contact with their relatives. According to the Home Office, about 15 per cent of prisoners are illiterate. Many are mentally handicapped or suffer from mental illness. Many have unstable work histories. In short, a high proportion of adult prisoners have been unable to attain a stable life at home or at work. Their personal inadequacies derive in large part from the socio-economic conditions they have experienced. Imprisonment usually makes them more inadequate and adds to the catalogue of rejection and failure.

Regrettably, the profile of the prison population also reflects unfair treatment of certain groups by the criminal justice system. This is particularly true of the black community. Fourteen per cent of the male prison population, and 23 per cent of the female prison population, is black. It is in relation to young men that there is most concern about racial discrimination. This takes three forms: police targeting of black communities, which increases the likelihood of criminalisation of young blacks; tougher sentences (blacks receive longer prison sentences, despite having on average fewer previous convictions); and racial discrimination in prison.

Black people's distrust of the criminal justice system derives both from their experiences as victims of crime and from what happens when they appear in court. Home Office research has established that Asians are 50 times more likely than white people, and Afro-Caribbeans 36 times more likely, to be victims of racially motivated attacks. The proportion of victims of robbery and assault from ethnic minorities is much higher than for the population as a whole, and is increasing. Many incidents of racial harassment are never reported to the police.

Many black people also lack confidence in the courts, where they experience what the *Caribbean Times* has called a 'conveyor belt of injustice' although the evidence from research into racial bias is conflicting. The economic and social disadvantage suffered by black people is itself a cause of injustice in the courts. In making a bail decision, for example, the court will inevitably look at a defendant's employment status and home circumstances. Because black people are discriminated against in work and in housing, they necessarily stand less chance of getting bail.

A comprehensive system of ethnic monitoring of courts' decisions should be established to ensure that racist practices and assumptions are weeded out. We also need to ensure that there are very many more black magistrates and judges, lawyers and prosecutors, police, probation and prison officers.

The Home Office's record in attracting black prison staff is deplorable, although it has gone a long way to establish anti-racist policies. Each prison should have a race relations committee and a designated race relations officer. However, in many gaols this has been little more than a paper exercise. Work carried out on behalf of the Home Office has also revealed the extent to which racist views and attitudes are held amongst prison staff. Out of 100 prison officers interviewed, only 6 did not volunteer pejorative characterisations of black prisoners: noisy, belligerent, lazy, demanding, unintelligent. Two examples: 'They remind me of a monkey colony', and 'Look at us, we fought two world wars to prevent Britain becoming a German colony and now we're infested with West Indians' (*Race Relations in Prisons*, Elaine Gender and Elaine Player, Oxford, 1989).

Inequality in the treatment of blacks and whites is not the only example of the system treating some groups less favourably than others. Those who commit various forms of white-collar crime, many of whom are middle class, are less likely to be prosecuted, and less likely to be imprisoned if convicted. Middle-class youngsters who break the law are also more likely to get away with a caution from the police or a more lenient sentence. Many adolescent boys from all social groups go through a period of challenging authority by various kinds of deviant behaviour. Between 7 and 8 per cent of all boys aged between 14 and 18 were known offenders in 1987. After the age of 18 the proportion falls rapidly as boys become more responsible and mature. Sending youths of this age to custodial institutions is not a satisfactory solution. The reconviction rates for young male offenders (those aged under 21 on sentence) are depressingly high; in 1984 65 per cent were reconvicted within two years of discharge from prison. Custodial sentences are likely to reduce the chance of a more socially responsible attitude developing. We are actually helping to create adult criminals by the way we treat young offenders. The fact that the crime rate for young men is much higher than for young women is attributed in part to macho culture. It is then foolish to consign young male offenders to penal regimes, calculated to make them even more macho.

The size of the prison population

It was pointed out in the introduction how badly Britain compares with other European countries with respect to the proportion of its citizens in prison. The most depressing aspect of the British figures is that, unlike most other European countries, the number being sent to prison has been rising continuously until the past year, when there was a small decrease. The obvious explanation for the rise is that it is a reflection of rising crime rates, but this only accounts for part of the increase. The Crown Courts have been sentencing an increasing proportion of those found guilty to prison; and there have been more long sentences. The Home Office is currently projecting an increase of 2–3,000 custodial sentences per annum over the next three or four years.

The figures on imprisonment over the last five years are the clearest manifestation of the total failure to deal with the problem. Before trying to explain what has gone wrong, it is necessary to disaggregate the 49,000 people now in prison. The most striking statistic over the last 20 years is the growth in the numbers in prison on remand. In 1967 there were 3,100 remand prisoners; by 1988 there were 11,400. In 1967 remand prisoners constituted 9 per cent of the total prison population; by 1987 this had risen to 23 per cent. The composition of the prison population has altered over the last six years. The biggest growth is in the number sentenced for drugs offences, which has more than trebled. There has also been a growth in the numbers in prison for crimes of violence, for sexual offences, and for robbery. In contrast the numbers in prison for property crimes, including burglary, theft and handling stolen goods have gone down. However, this group still constitutes more than a third of sentenced prisoners. Finally, while women still constitute a tiny proportion of the prison population, the numbers have been going up at a faster rate than for men.

More recently, during the 1980s, most of the rise in the total prison population can also be accounted for by the growth in the numbers held on remand. Why has this happened? First, we must acknowledge that the Bail Act of 1976, which introduced a statutory presumption in favour of bail, has not tamed those magistrates who still seem to regard bail as a privilege rather than an entitlement. Second, the general rise in crime has put increased pressure on the courts. The likelihood of a defendant being granted bail has in fact marginally improved since the Bail Act, but this has been swamped by the increased number of cases.

But the main reason for the explosion in the remand population is the increasing delay in bringing cases to trial. Regrettably, the establishment of the Crown Prosecution Service seems to have done nothing to reduce delay. Nor does the CPS seem to have taken a particularly robust and independent view of police objections to bail. One reason for delay occurs when defendants elect trial by judge and jury over summary trial by magistrates, but magistrates are also to blame. In many cases they decline jurisdiction and send cases on to the Crown Court, only for the eventual sentence to be one within the powers of magistrates' courts. There is nothing new about 'the law's delay' – Hamlet refers to it. For remand prisoners it means what one Conservative MP has described as 'punishment before trial'. Yet if a remand prisoner is acquitted or the charges dropped there is no system of compensation – indeed no redress at all.

Turning from remand prisoners to those who have been

convicted, there are three reasons for the increase in the numbers in prison: a growth in the proportion of offenders given custodial sentences by the Crown Courts; longer sentences; and restrictions on the use of parole for long-term prisoners. The fact that we have become readier to send adults to prison over the last ten years is especially worrying. The government itself concedes that 'a spell in custody is not the most effective punishment' for less serious offenders and that 'the self-discipline and self-reliance which will prevent reoffending in the future' is unlikely to be acquired in prison. Many experts have been saying this for some time; the fact that the government has at last come round to agreeing is welcome.

The Criminal Justice Act of 1972 introduced community service as a new non-custodial sentence. Community Service Orders are supervised by the probation service and the courts specify the number of hours of service required. The UK introduced community service before other European countries, but many have followed our lead, and a number of them now make greater use of this type of sentence than the UK. About 31,000 orders are now made each year, representing a threefold increase since 1979. Of those undertaking orders in 1986, 44 per cent were aged between 17 and 20. Community service is thus central to attempts to reduce the 22 per cent of the prison population who are young offenders. The key question is whether the courts can be persuaded to make greater use of it for adult offenders as well. Another problem is to persuade sentencers to substitute community service for custody rather than using it as an alternative to a fine, a probation order or a suspended prison sentence.

There is plenty of scope to do this. For example, a substantial number of people serve short prison sentences every year for petty thieving from shops. It is extremely doubtful whether anything is gained from sending them to prison, or indeed whether 'nuisance' offenders including those with alcohol and drugs problems should end up in gaol. While burglary and theft can cause their victims considerable distress, and constitute more than a mere nuisance in many cases, they are rarely a threat to public safety. If the prison population is to be reduced, those who commit these offences must be given non-custodial sentences on a much larger scale. Community service has much to recommend it; 75 per cent of offenders complete their orders successfully and only 9 per cent commit a further offence during the course of an order. Moreover, there is evidence that the public favours community service. In a poll carried out by NOP for the Prison Reform Trust in 1982, 85 per cent of those questioned were in favour of a reduction in the prison population by increased use of community service. What needs to be recognised by the courts is that prison seriously damages personal relationships, threatens employment and leads to loss of accommodation in many cases. It also isolates offenders from the community and removes the opportunity of making them more aware of the consequences of their actions and of seeking some form of reparation. Instead, burglars and thieves are locked up with more serious offenders in an environment where reparation is impossible.

The government's Green Paper rightly points out the substantial range of options now available to the courts as alternatives to imprisonment. The problem is to persuade the judiciary to make greater use of them. The government has correctly identified what is wrong: too many people who do not constitute a danger to the public go to prison; prison is expensive and ineffective. In 1987 74,000 offenders received either a Community Service Order, probation or supervision order; 69,000 were given custodial sentences (this figure does not include fine defaulters who eventually went to prison).

It is, however, questionable whether the government's proposal for a new sentence is what is really needed to reduce the latter figure further. What is proposed is a new supervision and restriction order combining a whole variety of sanctions in a single measure, with a more powerful punitive element. These might include compensation to the victim, community service, residence at a hostel, attendance at a day centre, curfew or house arrest and tracking an offender's whereabouts. The danger of the proposal is that it may have the effect of further reducing the use of fines, and, more important, it is likely to downgrade the use of existing community-based sentences. The likelihood is that offenders who would have received sentences consisting of one or at the most two elements of this package will end up with many more. If this happens the size of the prison population could actually be increased. Exacting requirements in the new order could mean that a higher proportion of non-custodial sentences are breached because the offender fails to comply. Thus, even though someone originally diverted from prison has not committed another offence, he or she ends up being sent there because the combination of compulsory activity and restrictions is too great to cope with, and compliance with the order fails. If there were a system to ensure that the new supervision and restriction order were only to be used in those cases where a lengthy prison sentence is imposed, it would be quite another matter. No proposals to achieve this are made by the government.

The problem of the UK's excessive use of prison

sentences does not derive from a shortage of alternatives, but rather from the lack of statutory guidelines given to the courts. The discretionary powers judges and magistrates possess are enormous. It is hard to escape the conclusion that they do not currently exercise this discretion in a way which is conducive to a sensible and cost-effective approach to the problems of crime in our society. It must be recognised that judges and magistrates face many difficult decisions, and their training and experience are often inadequate. Moreover, these decisions are made in a climate of 'get tough on crime' speeches by ministers. The government has a responsibility to devise a better system, which must include greater limits on judicial discretion.

Two things demonstrate this better than anything else: the outrageous disparity in sentencing from one part of the country to another, and the increasing use of long and very long sentences. Regional variations in sentencing are in danger of becoming accepted as an unavoidable part of the process. They should be constantly monitored and reported on in the hope that wide dissemination of information about the injustice involved might affect the courts' behaviour. Home Office studies comparing how different courts deal with similar cases have thrown up some quite remarkable disparities. For example, one court sent 7 per cent of burglars to prison, another sent 47 per cent; one court fined 19 per cent and another 62 per cent. In one court 48 per cent of first offenders found guilty of shoplifting were fined, in another the proportion was 86 per cent. Far worse, fewer than one in 200 first offenders were sent to prison by one court, compared with as many as one in ten by another. There are similar variations in the granting of bail. A Prison Reform Trust analysis of bail statistics showed that in 1984 there was a

64 per cent chance of getting bail in Dorset, whereas in Bedfordshire it was 97 per cent.

The average length of sentence has been creeping up. This is a result of longer sentences in the Crown Courts, where the average increased from 16.6 months in 1982 to 19.2 months in 1987. Even a small average increase can have a substantial impact on the prison population. As Vivien Stern has pointed out, the overall increase from 1983 (10.9 months) to 1984 (11.1 months) was the equivalent of a year's imprisonment for 866 people – enough to fill a prison the size of Walton in Liverpool. Average figures do not reveal anything about particular categories. For example, on present trends the numbers in prison will include some 5,000 life-sentence prisoners by the end of the century, over double the number today. Longer sentences for drugs offences and sexual attacks are also changing the pattern of the prison population. This requires the development of new skills by prison staff. In particular, the rapid growth in the number of sex offenders behind bars has revealed how little is presently done by way of treatment or otherwise challenging their behaviour. Some 2,000 so-called Rule 43 prisoners (predominantly sex offenders) are currently segregated from the rest of the prison population for their own protection. Yet, confined in each other's company, the predominant atmosphere is one which confirms fantasy images of women and children rather than challenging them.

There is no evidence to support the view that long sentences constitute a more effective deterrent than shorter sentences. Home Office researchers studied the rate of robberies in Birmingham before and after an exemplary sentence of 20 years was given to a boy of 16 found guilty of violent robbery. It had no effect at all, in spite of the highly-publicised trial and sentence. Most people have little idea what the length of sentence usually is for particular crimes, and serious crimes involving violence are often committed by people in an emotional and irrational state of mind where calculations about how long they might spend in prison are hardly likely to be made. All the evidence also suggests that longer sentences are no more effective than shorter sentences with respect to reconviction.

As the Home Office itself advises in its handbook for magistrates: 'The research evidence ... suggests that within the realistic range of choice, imposing particular sentences, or particularly severe sentences, has a very limited effect on crime levels. The probability of arrest and conviction is likely to deter potential offenders, whereas the perceived severity of the ensuing penalties has little effect. No realistic increase in prison terms would make a substantial impact on crime rates simply by virtue of locking up the particular offenders caught, convicted and sentenced' (*The Sentence of the Court*, HMSO, 1986).

Finally, changing the rules about when people can be released from prison has a more immediate effect on prison numbers than most other measures. The numbers in prison have recently been affected by changes in the use of parole. At the lower end, many more prisoners have become eligible for parole. At the upper end, the rules have become much more restrictive – to all intents and purposes parole has been abolished for sentences of over five years. The net effect has been to reduce the prison population by about 1,500–2,000.

Parole was originally introduced in 1967 as a means of reducing the prison population, although it was rationalised in terms of the appropriate 'treatment' of prisoners. They were to be released when their 'training' in prison had reached completion. Since training in prison is singularly lacking, this reasoning has subsequently been dismissed by most informed commentators as absurd. Nevertheless, it is probably true that adding parole to remission has been an effective way of reducing numbers in prison. Remission is granted automatically, although it can be lost for misbehaviour. It is granted after a prisoner has served two thirds of his or her sentence when the sentence is longer than 12 months, and after serving half the sentence when it is 12 months or less. One-half remission was introduced as another desperate measure to reduce the prison population. Parole is granted on a discretionary basis after a minimum of one third of a sentence has been served, and has various conditions attached. The extent to which parole is effective must be qualified by one important consideration: judges may increase the length of sentences to take parole into account.

The parole system is currently under review. It is likely to be drastically reduced in its scope. This would be a victory for those who have argued that it is an unjust system. Prisoners are subject to administrative rather than legal procedures; decisions are made in private; no reasons are given for them. Prisoners have neither the right to be heard nor the right to be told why an application has been refused. But the reason why the future of parole is uncertain is that the government has messed about with it so much that it is now riddled with anomalies. Moreover, by virtually abolishing it for prisoners serving sentences of more than five years, it has removed the hope of earlier release from these prisoners and has thereby increased the problems of the prison service in managing this group. It was abolished retrospectively as a 'get tough' measure by Leon Brittan.

Many long-term prisoners thus had their sentences extended well beyond what they had expected, with a corresponding increase in tension in the prisons.

Leon Brittan's policy has had one other perverse effect. Short-sentence and non-violent prisoners are compulsorily supervised on release under the terms of a parole licence. Long-sentence and violent prisoners receive no help or supervision on release (although they may need it much more) because they are now released at the end of their sentences, not earlier on parole.

Panicking about prison numbers and overcrowding in 1984, the government lowered the length of sentence eligible for parole. At face value there might seem little wrong with this. In practice it has meant that there has been little difference in actual time served on sentences between 9 and 18 months. Just as the variation in sentences for similar crimes from one area to another is a scandalous lottery, so too is the amount of time spent in prison by many serving these 'middle term' sentences.

If the experience of prison were more constructive, there would be less need for concern about the numbers of people locked up in British gaols and the vagaries of how long the individual offender ends up spending 'inside'. It is because prisons are degrading and ultimately destructive for those who are sent to languish in them that it is so urgent to keep them out wherever possible.

Conditions in prison

A visit to a closed prison for the first time is a deeply disturbing experience. It is an assault on the senses: the stench of stale cabbage; the banging of cell doors on the echoing landings; the sight of three men to a cell built for one; airlessness; clanking keys; flaking paint. The most pervasive impression of all derives not, however, from the deplorable physical conditions, but from the sense of hopeless inactivity. In no other human institution are people to be found in such large numbers doing nothing for such long stretches of time. Whether locked in their cells or out 'on association' there is an overwhelming sense of purposelessness and of enforced sloth amongst the inmates. Those employed to guard them also appear to be victims of the system, giving the impression of spending much of their time standing around, with little sign of meaningful activity or communication with their charges.

There are two aspects of life in prison which will make future historians amazed that an otherwise tolerant and humane society could have shirked prison reform for so long. The first is the disgraceful squalor of the physical conditions; the second is the repressive nature of the regime. The buildings in which many prisons are housed are unfit to live in; they are dark, dismal, in a state of disrepair and, above all, insanitary. The practice of slopping out has been condemned as repulsive and degrading by every commentator and every authority from the Chief Inspector of Prisons to the Prison Officers' Association. It is remarkable that the government has concentrated so much investment in building 28 new prisons, with the result that slopping out will probably continue in the older ones into the next century. Slopping out in any form is indefensible; slopping out in the overcrowded conditions of three to a cell built for one is a denial of the most basic human privacy. The general lack of privacy, in which no man sharing a cell can ever be alone, is dehumanising. The restrictions on having baths or showers and the infrequent provision of changes of clothes, the lack of access to a lavatory, all contribute to the brutalising of prison inmates.

However, the daily regime to which prisoners are subjected is even more damaging than the physical conditions. Many prisoners are locked in their cells for hours at a stretch – in some cases for as much as 23 hours a day. Individuals who are a threat to society because of their violent and anti-social behaviour must expect to be denied their freedom. But locking them up in tiny cells is not the answer. Yet it happens – not just to this group, but to thousands of others who are no more than a nuisance to society. In local prisons and remand centres young men are cooped up with a couple of strangers, with grossly inadequate opportunities for exercise. It is hardly surprising that the atmosphere in overcrowded prisons can become explosive. Yet the Home Office has been singularly unsuccessful in redistributing prisoners from grossly overcrowded local prisons to other prisons where overcrowding is not a problem. Many prisons do not allow their inmates to eat in association. Instead they must take their food and eat it in their cells. It is shocking that this is happening even in young offenders' establishments. Boys of 17 and 18 already locked up for most of the day are shut up to eat, because this is easier to supervise.

Prisons ought to provide opportunities for education and training, which many offenders desperately need to help them obtain jobs when they are released. They ought to provide some challenge to prisoners to set themselves objectives, to master skills and to acquire new knowledge. Above all they should help prisoners become less dependent and more self-disciplined, and as a result acquire a more positive self-image. Most prisons fail hopelessly in this respect. Even young offenders sit idle in prisons where facilities have been provided. Feltham Young Offenders' Establishment, for example, is a brand new prison, with workshops and instructors. Its workshops have been empty for substantial periods whilst its instructors stand about waiting for 'clients'. Meanwhile under-educated and untrained youngsters are locked in their cells because of difficulties in deploying prison officers to oversee their periods in the workshop. It is a scandalous waste of human and physical resources.

If prisoners are to survive as law-abiding citizens when they are released, it is essential that they maintain contact with their families. Prison regulations provide for a minimum number of visits of a minimum duration, allowing individual prisons discretion to increase them. Unfortunately the combination of overcrowding and the organisational problems this creates, and coping with the different arrangements for visiting of remand prisoners, results in many local prisons providing for little or no visiting above the minimum. This means prisoners over the age of 21 have one half-hour visit every 28 days and those under 21 a half-hour every 14 days. This amounts to 6½ hours and 13 hours per annum respectively. The psychological effects on families and prisoners alike are enormous. Many relatives have to travel considerable distances to see prisoners, making the short time allocated per visit particularly harsh. Remand prisoners are allowed daily visits of fifteen minutes, an absurdly short time. It would surely be less frustrating for prisoners and relatives alike if more time per visit with fewer visits was allowed. Women in prison suffer more than men because of these arrangements, as the small number of women in prison means that women's prisons are widely dispersed. Since many women in prison have children, the psychological damage caused by the severance of family relationships is especially acute.

There are limited possibilities for home leave, but the numbers eligible are a very small proportion of the total inmate population. Compared with many other countries Britain is extremely conservative about home leave. It also compares badly with countries such as Canada, Sweden and the Netherlands with respect to the frequency, length and conditions of visits. The total lack of privacy in which visits take place in British prisons is yet another deprivation imposed by the system.

Maintaining contact with families and friends through letters is also constrained by oppressive rules. Sentenced prisoners are allowed to send one statutory letter a week, postage paid by the authorities, and one additional letter, postage paid out of their earnings. They may be allowed to write extra letters where this is deemed necessary for the welfare of the prisoner or his or her family. Letters cannot normally be more than four sides in length and must usually be written on lined prison paper with a number in the corner. All letters, incoming or outgoing, are censored by prison officers. This is true of remand prisoners' letters too. Only in Category C (for low-risk offenders) and open prisons are the rules more relaxed. There, letters are opened to check for contraband but not read except in a 5 per cent random sample in the case of Category C prisons. Unfortunately, Home Office attempts to relax censorship have been obstructed by the Prison Officers' Association. The fact that letters are scrutinised on such a large scale means that many prisoners may feel inhibited about expressing their feelings openly to their families and friends. This can only add to the distance between them and make the re-establishment of close ties when prisoners are released more difficult. In this respect, as in the case of visiting, the regime in British prisons is more punitive than in many other comparable countries. In some countries, including Canada, the USA and Holland prisoners have access to telephones. They are also available in Scottish prisons. A recent concession has been made in England and Wales allowing outgoing calls in Category C and open prisons. Elsewhere prisoners cannot phone their families.

Security considerations appear to loom so large in the minds of those in authority that attempts to liberalise the regime always fail. It must surely be desirable to accept an element of risk in the interests of the rehabilitation of prisoners. Considerations of cost are also relevant. It is an absurd misuse of prison officers' time to read low-security prisoners' letters.

Even a short account of conditions in prison would not be complete without reference to the disparity between the regime for remand prisoners and the rest. In spite of the fact that those remanded in custody have not been found guilty, and may never be, their regime is in many respects worse than that of convicted prisoners. In a prison such as Wormwood Scrubs, where there are substantial numbers of remand prisoners as well as those convicted of serious offences who will be in prison for several years, remand prisoners are locked in their cells for longer hours; their conditions are more likely to be overcrowded; and they have no access to any education or training even though many of them are young and some of them may be in prison for months. In 1970 the average stay was 23 days; by 1987 it had risen to 56 days. Many remand prisoners (2,810 in 1987) are found not guilty or have the charges against them dropped. Many more are eventually given non-custodial

43

sentences (nearly 18,000 in 1987). Women in particular suffer from this system; one third of men remanded in custody get a non-custodial sentence; two thirds of women do. Many women on remand are sent to prison merely for reports on their medical condition or social circumstances. The system is transparently unjust. It also leads to its miserable victims committing suicide more often than those who have been sentenced to prison. There have also been serious riots in remand prisons, such as Risley, where anger, frustration and a deep-seated sense of injustice have eventually boiled over.

The sad conclusion is that conditions in most prisons are not only bad, but deteriorating. A recent study compared the situation in 1970/72 and 1985/87. Its authors found in a 'different but representative and comparable group of five prisons for adult males' that while sanitary conditions have been improved, 'on most measures including access to those facilities, the recent study revealed consistently worse regimes than the earlier study in spite of major improvements in staff:prisoner ratios'. The higher security prisons, which generally have better facilities, 'now more closely resemble the local prisons of fifteen years ago'. They found more crowding, less time out of cells, less association time, and fewer prisoners participating in education than formerly. They conclude: 'To discuss the problems of the prison system in terms of overcrowded local prisons is too simple. The apparent deterioration in core areas of the regime is on a major scale and has bitten deep into the training prisons . . . The picture becomes very bleak indeed' (King and McDermott, 1989).

Release from Prison

Every year almost 100,000 people in this country are released after serving prison sentences. The fact that so many of them are reconvicted is not altogether surprising given their circumstances on release. If any of us found ourselves on the streets tomorrow without accommodation or a job, perhaps without family or friends, and with the equivalent of one week's benefits in our pockets, how would we manage?

Many ex-prisoners are homeless when released – the estimates range from one quarter to one half depending upon the area of the country. Because of the lack of accommodation, ex-prisoners face further problems in claiming social security benefits, finding work, or establishing themselves in a normal life. Not surprisingly, homelessness is a major influence upon re-offending. A Home Office study of petty offenders carried out 20 years ago (amazingly, the Home Office has carried out no subsequent study) showed that petty offenders who were homeless had a reconviction rate almost *three* times that of those who were not homeless.

Ex-prisoners also suffer employment problems. Again, it is remarkable that no accurate statistics exist, but it is known that most prisoners are released to life on the dole. Where ex-prisoners are successful in finding work, it is usually at a lower level than before their sentences. Few prisoners have a job arranged on release, a problem which has been exacerbated by the high unemployment rates of the last decade. Many employers are reluctant to take on people who have been in prison for fear that they will be unreliable. This becomes a self-fulfilling prophecy, since people without a job are much more likely to drift back to crime.

The financial situation facing an ex-prisoner also contributes to the likelihood of re-offending. On release most prisoners receive a discharge grant which amounts to one week's Income Support (or more for those who are homeless). However, prisoners are not paid any Income Support until a fortnight after they leave prison. Ex-prisoners can of course apply to the DSS for a crisis loan from the social fund, and are amongst the priority groups for community care grants. However, the process is time-consuming and fails to meet the special financial needs of prisoners on release. For example, in many areas it is impossible to secure rented accommodation without putting down a substantial deposit in advance. A discharge grant closer to the average weekly wage is needed if ex-prisoners are to be in a position to tackle their financial problems on release.

The Prison Department's 'mission statement', that the duty of the prison service is to help prisoners 'lead law-abiding and useful lives in custody and after release', implies that preparation for release should receive a high priority. In order to sort out their problems and to prepare effectively for release, prisoners need access to a range of advice and support services: generally speaking, the same services which are available to the general public. This implies access to employment and education schemes and to advisory agencies like Citizens' Advice Bureaus, housing and legal aid centres. It would also help if prisoners could keep in touch with families and friends while they are inside. Improvements to prisoners' rights – such as allowing access to telephones, reducing the censorship of mail, and dropping restrictions on the number of letters they can write – are all more relevant to rehabilitation after release than they may appear at first.

Recommendations for Reform

The changes that are needed have been implicit in much of the account so far. Some of them need to be made more explicit.

It is in some ways understandable that the government has embarked on a prison building programme. There must be a solution to overcrowding, and something must be done about the insanitary conditions and the lack of other facilities, for example for exercise, particularly in the local prisons. It is, however, complete folly to rely so much on the vastly expensive solution of building more prisons. New building in some ways compounds the problem. The more places there are available, the more likely they are to be filled. The pressure to find alternatives to gaol is relieved. It is on alternatives that the government should focus its attention.

However difficult it may be to persuade judges and magistrates to give up some of their discretion, this must be done. A small step in the direction of reducing judges' and magistrates' discretion was taken with the Bail Act of 1976. Unless there are good reasons not to, the courts are required to grant bail. The Act did bring down the numbers in prison on remand, although those numbers have since crept up again. Without the Act they would undoubtedly be higher. But more needs to be done with respect to bail, given that one third of those imprisoned before trial do not get a prison sentence. First, the Act needs to be more rigorously applied, so that the courts are less inclined to find or accept reasons for not giving bail. Second, the system of bail hostels for those without a fixed address should be expanded. Third, remand prisoners should be brought to trial much sooner. There should be limits on the amount of time spent in prison on remand, especially for non-violent offenders. The Scottish system has a limit of 110 days; no extension is allowed unless the defence has caused the delay. One of the few things Leon Brittan got right as Home Secretary was to initiate an experiment in trial deadlines. These have now spread to most parts of the country, but the limits are still too long and do not have the force of law. A shorter limit should now be introduced in England and Wales, perhaps with a differential for violent and non-violent offences. A statutory requirement to hear cases more quickly should be uncontroversial. Nevertheless, opposition to it by the courts has prevented it.

Resistance to the introduction of a coherent sentencing policy involving statutory guidelines for magistrates and judges is, it appears, even greater. Yet without a fundamental change of this sort, there seems little hope that we shall be able to crack the problem of too many people in prison. There is no shortage of alternatives to imprisonment. The problem is to get judges and magistrates to use them. Probation day centres, detoxification centres and community service orders have all been underused. Where they are used, it is frequently as a substitute for fines rather than for prison.

Various suggestions have been put forward for some kind of formal mechanism to formulate sentencing policy. For example, a Sentencing Council has been proposed. It might consist of a variety of experts and experienced people including prison governors, senior Home Office officials, probation officers, academics and judges and magistrates. Its job would be to plan and co-ordinate policy on sentencing and to provide realistic guidelines. In 1981 the House of Commons Select Committee on Home Affairs proposed something similar, but with a rather broader remit. A National Criminal Policy Committee would plan criminal policy, making use of expert advice and research findings. It would include policy design and resource allocation for crime prevention as well as sentencing policy and its implementation.

The precise nature of the structure is in some ways unimportant. What is vital is that it should set out clear principles on which sentences, particularly non-custodial sentences, can be calculated. It should make clear that prison is a last resort to be confined to dangerous criminals and those who seriously undermine the social order. It should also clearly set out the costs of different sentences, reviewing them and keeping them up to date. A bland disregard for the costs of dealing with offenders by those imposing sentences cannot be allowed to continue, any more than it can be allowed in relation to doctors pre-scribing drugs for their patients.

Differences in the costs of custodial and non-custodial sentences are startling. In 1987–88 the figures ranged from £184 per person per week in adult open prisons to £557 per week in dispersal prisons which house high-security prisoners. To spend an average of £275 per week locking people up when many of them could be subjected to less damaging and cheaper sanctions is an absurd misuse of resources. It costs approximately the same to supervise someone on probation for a whole year as to keep them in a local prison for three and a half weeks. It costs less to supervise a young offender on a Community Service Order for a whole year (most orders are for less than this) than to keep him in prison for two and a half weeks. The most expensive non-custodial sentences, such as probation hostels, are little more than half the cost of prison; the average weekly cost of prison is twenty times more than

49

probation or community service. Fines actually raise money: £185 million in 1987–88. It is incomprehensible that a government so concerned to reduce public expenditure has done so little in response to facts such as these.

Little progress has been made in keeping people out of prison who should never have gone there in the first place. Soliciting is no longer an imprisonable offence, nor is sleeping rough or begging. Other offences could be added to this list, such as shoplifting or fine defaulting. There are also certain categories of prisoner who should not have ended up in gaol. There is a large group of persistent petty offenders whose crimes are a nuisance, but not a threat to other individuals or society. Many are socially inadequate single men without family or friends and little secure employment. They require help and support from various services, including housing and probation, rather than being given repeated short sentences and cluttering up the local prisons. Another category which should not in most cases be in prison is the mentally ill. People who suffer from psychiatric disorders of various kinds commit crimes as a direct result of their illness. Rather than languishing in prison, they need psychiatric help from skilled professionals. Women's prisons are particularly likely to contain a high proportion of disturbed offenders who should be elsewhere.

Women's imprisonment, it was predicted in the sixties, would gradually disappear. In fact it has grown. Over half the women in prison have dependent children. Women are more likely to be first offenders or to be held on remand than men; they are less likely to have long histories of offending. Prison appears to have a particularly destructive effect on women; it is also very costly to society, because frequently their children need to be cared for by the state. Many women in prison should be dealt with by non-custodial methods.

Reference has already been made to young people in custody. As long ago as 1969 the Children and Young Persons' Act envisaged the phasing out of custody for children under the age of 17. This has not happened; in 1987–88 there were 3,200 children aged 14 to 16 sent into custody. The 1988 Criminal Justice Act has phased out the dual system of detention centres focusing on 'short sharp shocks' and the more training-orientated youth custody centres. The Act has introduced a single generic sentence in a Young Offender Institution, as they are now called. However, this does not address the question of whether any child should be sent to an institution where prison conditions operate. Some progress has been made in restricting the courts' ability to sentence children and young people to custody. For example, they cannot remand youngsters under 17 to prison except where a very serious or violent offence has been committed. That age limit should now be raised to 18. The prison system is not the right way of dealing with difficult children.

Unlike a number of European countries, Britain has no Ministry of Justice in which the courts and the prisons could come under the same government department. As a result, those who make decisions about how offenders are treated and who goes to prison are part of a quite different organisation to those who decide the resources allocated to prisons and other penal institutions and the nature of their regimes. Another difference between the British system and that of a number of our European neighbours is that there is no professional judiciary. French lawyers, for example, decide early in their careers whether they wish to be advocates or judges. They then work their way through the lower courts gaining experience, before promotion to more senior judicial positions. In Britain most judges are not appointed until their late forties or possibly later, having until then spent their careers as advocates.

Both these differences pose problems for the British system. First, the structure is not conducive to developing a more efficient use of resources. The Home Office's budget is quite separate from that of the Lord Chancellor's department; the latter has no particular incentive to put pressure on the judiciary to consider cheaper and more efficient alternatives to prison. The Home Office, on the other hand, is a victim of the doctrine of the preservation of the independence of the judiciary at all cost. It has little direct leverage in what has become a system demand-led by the courts. Second, many judges have no first-hand knowledge of the penal system when they are appointed, and unlike Continental judges they have not been able to build up experience of sentencing. Judicial training is now provided, but is hardly adequate for the task. Moreover, because of the sensitivities of the judges, training operates under the silly euphemism of 'judicial studies programmes'. The more conservative and resistant judges are about such matters as training and accepting statutory guidelines on sentencing, the greater the need will become to consider more fundamental change, along the lines of an expert professional judiciary.

Sentencing policy is the key to reducing the numbers in prison. It is also the key to improving prison conditions. Conditions deteriorate dramatically with overcrowding. Disgraceful local prisons like Reading cannot be closed while so many offenders are being given custodial sentences. However, other steps can be taken to mitigate some of the worst aspects of life in prison.

First and foremost, the length of time prisoners are locked in their cells should be reduced. There should be more opportunities for education and training for all prisoners, including those on remand. The all-too frequent phenomenon of empty classrooms in prisons because of problems in the deployment of staff should be resolved. It is also astonishing that prison workshops have been closed and that so little has been done to extend the range of work possible. The output of prison workshops has gone down by 60 per cent, and the hours of work available have been dropping each year. The frustration and boredom that results from inactivity are likely to create problems of control which would not arise if prisoners had more to do. A constructive working environment is likely to make it possible to reduce the effort that goes into security, rather than increasing it. It is more humane than locking prisoners up. It can also give prisoners some sense of purpose and reduce the feeling of dependence which hours of being idle generates. A regime allowing more time for prisoners to work is therefore of benefit to both staff and inmates.

It was emphasised in an earlier section how important it is to allow greater contact between prisoners and their families. The practice of reading incoming and outgoing letters should be stopped; the POA cannot be allowed to dictate the rules on such matters. There should be improved facilities for visiting and greater possibilities for home leave.

Imposing living conditions which are likely to undermine self-respect, because of dirty underwear, too few baths per week, having to defecate in a bucket in front of others, is hardly constructive. The regime of prisons should be geared to increasing prisoners' self-respect, not to destroying it. Allowing male prisoners to wear their own clothes rather than undermining individuality by imposing uniforms is a concession which should be made and could be achieved without much cost. Above all, slopping out should be ended and washing facilities should be improved.

In summary, Britain has a disastrously expensive and inhumane penal system, which is being compounded by a huge injection of resources into building more prisons. Placing so much emphasis on building prisons is a sad reflection on the innovative abilities of the government. A little more imagination, rather more attention to the evidence in front of them, and greater political courage would have led ministers down a quite different path. It would have led them to a sustained effort to reduce substantially the prison population. It *can* be done, as the Dutch and West German experiences demonstrate. Substantial sums of public money could be saved, even after investing more resources in Community Service Orders and other non-custodial sanctions. Having fewer men and women in prison would make it easier to provide a more humane regime, recognising that prison must and does involve an element of retribution, but with the fundamental objective of the rehabilitation of prisoners.

By their actions some men and a few women in all societies forfeit their right to their liberty. Prisons will always be needed for the small number of human beings who cannot control their aggression and who behave violently towards others, or whose uncontrollable greed undermines the society in which they operate. They should not be used as dumping grounds for mentally ill or socially inadequate petty offenders, nor for undisciplined and immature adolescents and young men, who given careful handling and a little help, will in most cases grow out of their criminal behaviour and become law-abiding citizens.

The task is clear. I challenge the Home Secretary to embark on a programme to halve the number of people in prison by the year 2000. If this were achieved the 1990s would be the most memorable decade in the history of penal policy in Britain since Winston Churchill set himself the target of reducing the number of short prison sentences by 'at least a third, perhaps more' 80 years ago.

Bibliography

David Downes, *Contrasts in Tolerance*, Oxford University Press, 1988

Elaine Gender and Elaine Player, *Race Relations in Prison*, Oxford University Press, 1989

HMSO
   Audit Commission, *The Probation Service: Promoting Value for Money*, 1989
   Criminal Justice: A Working Paper, rev. ed. 1986
   National Audit Office, *Home Office and Property Services Agency: Programme for the Provision of Prison Places*, HC 135, 1985/86 Parliamentary Session
   Private Sector Involvement in the Remand System, Cm 434, July 1988
   Punishment, Custody and the Community, Cm 424, July 1988
   The Sentence of the Court, 1986

Roy King and Kathleen McDermott, 'British Prisons 1970–1987: The Ever-Deepening Crisis', *British Journal of Criminology*, 29, 2, Spring 1989

Prison Reform Trust, *Comments on the Green Paper; Punishment, Custody and the Community*, January 1989

Vivien Stern, *Bricks of Shame*, Penguin, 1987

About the Author

TESSA BLACKSTONE is Master of Birkbeck College, and a Labour member of the House of Lords. She is also Chairman of the Board of Trustees of the Institute for Public Policy Research and of the BBC General Advisory Council and is a Trustee of the Prison Reform Trust. She is the author of a number of books and many articles on social and education policy. Her latest book (with William Plowden) *Inside the Think Tank: Advising the Cabinet 1971–83*, on the Central Policy Review Staff, was published in 1988.

CHATTO
CounterBlasts

Also available in bookshops now:-

No. 1 Jonathan Raban — **God, Man & Mrs Thatcher**
No. 2 Paul Foot — **Ireland:** Why Britain Must Get Out
No. 3 John Lloyd — **A Rational Advance for the Labour Party**
No. 4 Fay Weldon — **Sacred Cows:** A Portrait of Britain, post-Rushdie, pre-Utopia
No. 5 Marina Warner — **Into the Dangerous World**
No. 6 William Shawcross — **Kowtow!**
No. 7 Ruth Rendell and Colin Ward — **Undermining the Central Line**
No. 8 Mary Warnock — **Universities:** Knowing Our Minds
No. 9 Sue Townsend — **Mr Bevan's Dream**
No. 10 Christopher Hitchens — **The Monarchy**

Forthcoming Chatto CounterBlasts

No. 12 Douglas Dunn — **Poll Tax: The Fiscal Fake**
No. 13 Ludovic Kennedy — **Euthanasia**
No. 14 Adam Mars-Jones — **Venus Envy**
No. 15 Adam Lively — **Bastion Britain**
No. 16 Peter Fuller — **Left High and Dry**
No. 17 Margaret Drabble — **Safe as Houses**
No. 18 Ronald Dworkin — **A Bill of Rights for Britain**

Plus pamphlets from Michael Holroyd, Hanif Kureishi, Michael Ignatieff and Susannah Clapp

If you want to join in the debate, and if you want to know more about **CounterBlasts**, the writers and the issues, then write to:

Random Century Group, Freepost WC5066, Dept MH, London SW1V 2YY